A COOL BRUSHBACK

Lindy Kelly

illustrated by Courtney Hopkinson

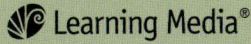
Learning Media®

"We're going on vacation!" Dad told Darnel and Tiana at breakfast. "Uncle Calvin said we can use his cabin up at the lake again. Do you two remember the last time we stayed?"

Tiana nodded. "I do!" she said. "We went swimming and fishing. Hey, Darnel, remember when we saw that bear and her cubs?"

Darnel shrugged and kept on eating.

"What's wrong, Darnel?" asked Mom. "We thought you'd love to go to the lake again."

Darnel looked at his parents. How could he explain?

"Will you take me fishing, Darnel?" asked Tiana, her eyes wide with excitement. "Do you think we'll see bears again?"

"No," said Darnel, "because I'm not going." He went to pack his books for school and left without saying good-bye.

At the bus stop, Darnel's friend Stevie was waiting. A couple of girls walked by on the other side of the street. They waved at Stevie, and he nodded back. Stevie had only started at Darnel's school a month ago, and already he was the coolest guy in their class. He was smart and good at baseball, and he had all the latest gear. No wonder he was popular. Best of all, Stevie had chosen Darnel to hang out with.

The school bus pulled up, and Stevie and Darnel sat at the back.

"What are you doing this weekend?" Stevie asked, looking out the window.

"Nothing much. What about you?" Darnel replied.

"I've bought a new computer game. Maybe you could come over."

"Great!" said Darnel, hoping his parents didn't have a family outing in mind.

At lunch, Darnel and Stevie sat with their friends in the cafeteria. Darnel asked everyone what they were doing for their vacation.

"I'm visiting my cousins," said Manuel.

"I'm helping Dad paint the den," said Jacob.

"I've bought a new computer game," said Stevie.

"Cool," said everyone.

"What about you, Darnel?" asked Stevie.

Darnel shrugged. "We're going to the lake, but I don't want to go," he said.

"Why don't you want to come on vacation with us?" Darnel's dad asked that night.

"I just want to be with my friends. It's not cool to go on vacation with your parents and your little sister." Darnel glanced up and saw that his dad looked hurt.

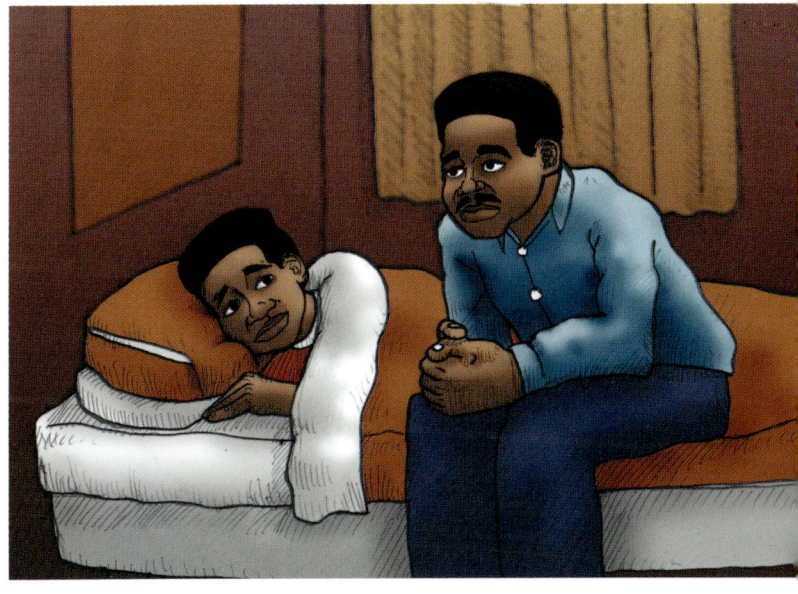

"I see. Well, goodnight." Dad's voice sounded sad. He patted Darnel's shoulder and left the room. Darnel lay awake, feeling bad.

The next day, Stevie said, "I was just thinking how lucky you are, going to the lake."

"Why?" Darnel asked. He couldn't believe it.

"Well, I haven't been on a family vacation since Dad died," Stevie said.

"I'll ask my folks if you can come with us," said Darnel. "It'll be great. We can take the boat out and go fishing."

Stevie smiled. "Sounds like a cool vacation."